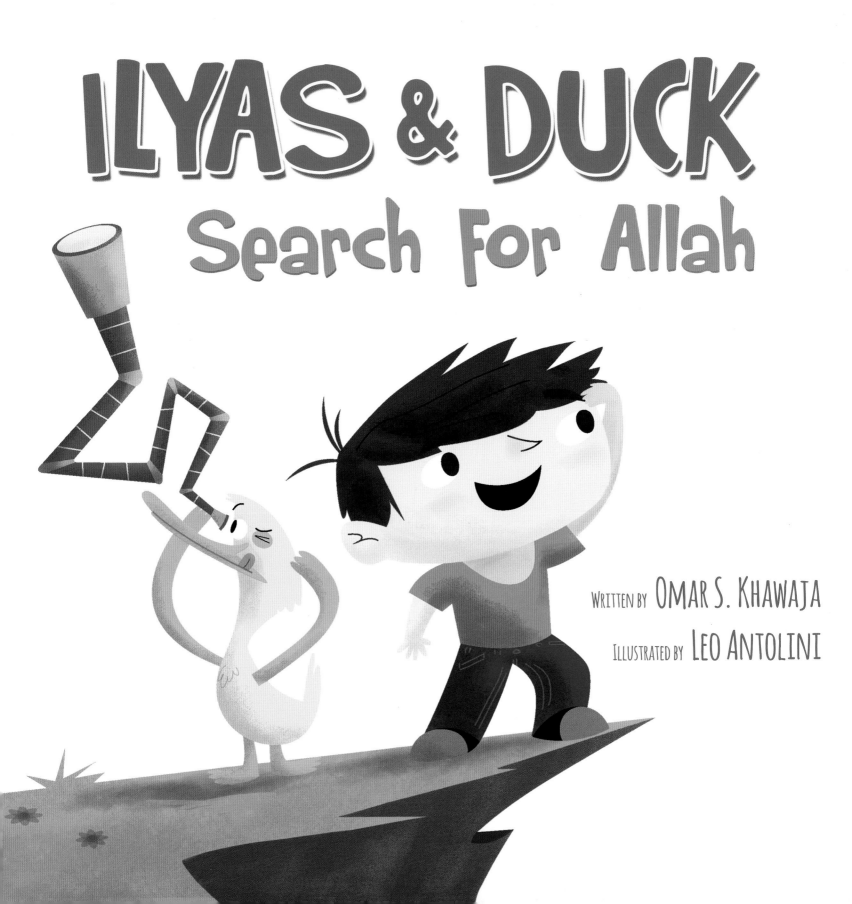

ILYAS & DUCK
Search For Allah

WRITTEN BY OMAR S. KHAWAJA

ILLUSTRATED BY LEO ANTOLINI

To my kids, Daamin, Ali and Yasmeen:
May you never outgrow your innocent sense of wonder.
- O.S.K.

A special thank you to my wife Nadia for putting up with me.

LBK Books
Hatched in Washington D.C.
www.LittleBigKids.com

Printed in China
This product conforms to CPSIA 2008
First Printing, 2012

Library of Congress Control Number: 2012913563

ISBN 978-0-9850728-1-0

5 6 7 8 9 21 20 19 18

Verily in the heavens and the earth, are Signs for those who believe.
And in the creation of yourselves and the fact that animals are scattered
(through the earth), are Signs for those of assured faith.

- The Qur'an: Surah 45 (*verses 3 and 4*)

One night, Ilyas snuggled into bed and thanked Allah for his mother, father and best friend Duck.

Then as he slowly drifted to sleep, Ilyas began to wonder...

"Where is Allah?"

Early the next morning, Duck noticed Ilyas
in the backyard staring up at the sky.

"What are you looking at?" asked Duck.
"I'm looking for Allah," replied Ilyas.

"Hmmm..."

"Here, try these binoculars.
They help you see things that are far away."

Ilyas looked through the binoculars but all he could see were a few puffy clouds and a plane flying by.

"You won't see Allah with those binoculars," said the Hoopoe sitting on the branch of a tree nearby.

"What do you mean?" asked Ilyas. But the Hoopoe didn't answer. It just flew away.

"Maybe we need to be closer to the sky to see Allah," suggested Duck.

Ilyas agreed.

So they put on their backpacks and climbed to the peak of the tallest mountain.

That's where they saw...

an Alpine Ibex!

"We're looking for Allah," said Ilyas.
"Do you know where we can find Him?"

"Yes," replied the long-horned goat. "Allah is all around us. He made the mountains as tall as can be. But you can't see Allah like you can see me."

"What do you mean?" asked Ilyas. But the Alpine Ibex didn't answer. It just trotted away.

"Maybe Allah is somewhere in the ocean," suggested Duck.

Ilyas agreed.

So they put on their scuba gear and dove to the bottom of the deepest ocean.

That's where they saw...

an Anglerfish!

"We're looking for Allah," said Ilyas.
"Do you know where we can find Him?"

"Yes," replied the sharp-toothed fish. "Allah is all around us. He gave me gills so I can breathe. But you can't see Allah like you can see me."

"What do you mean?" asked Ilyas. But the Anglerfish didn't answer. It just swam away.

"Maybe Allah is in a rainforest," suggested Duck.

Ilyas agreed.

So they put on their safari outfits and hiked into the warm and wet rainforest.

That's where they saw...

a Mandrill!
"We're looking for Allah," said Ilyas.
"Do you know where we can find Him?"

"Yes," replied the colorful monkey. "Allah is all around us. He gave me colors that make me unique. But you can't see Allah like you can see me."

"What do you mean?" asked Ilyas. But the Mandrill didn't answer. It just swung away.

"Maybe Allah is in outer space," suggested Duck.

Ilyas agreed.

So they climbed into their rocketship
and blasted off to space.

That's where they saw...

millions of stars in space and the beautiful earth below.

"Wow, this is amazing!" exclaimed Ilyas.
"It sure is." replied Duck. "But where is Allah?"

"I think I know the answer!" replied Ilyas. "Now I understand what all the animals were trying to tell us about Allah."

"What do you mean?" asked Duck.

Well Duck, *Allah* is the one who made the universe and everything else that we see. From the mountains to the oceans, even you and me.

But we can't see Allah the same way I can see you. We see Allah through all His creations. And through them we believe Allah to be true."

That night Ilyas laid in bed smiling. He had learned that Allah's signs were all around him.

Then he closed his eyes and fell fast asleep.

Hoopoe [hoo-poo]

Hoopoes are named for the "hoo-hoo-hoo" call they make. They are also known for the beautiful feathered crown on their heads. Did you know that the Hoopoe is mentioned in the Quran [27:20, 27:22]? Awesome!

Alpine Ibex [al-pahyn ahy-beks]

Alpine Ibex are extremely good climbers. Clearly not afraid of heights, they live in steep, rocky regions along the snow line in altitudes as high as 6,000 - 11,000 feet. Amazing!

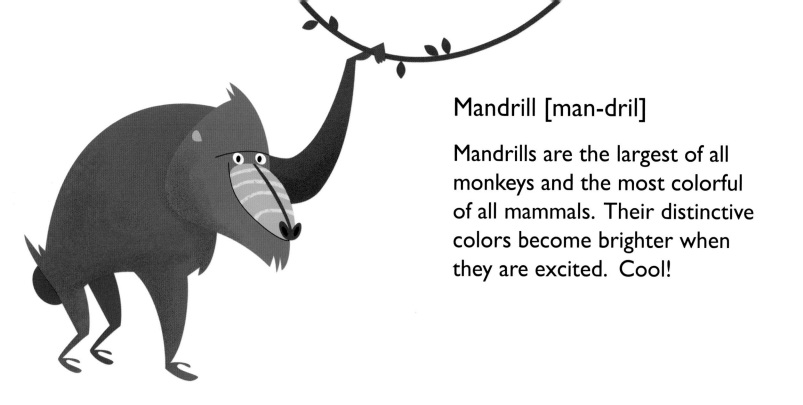

Mandrill [man-dril]

Mandrills are the largest of all monkeys and the most colorful of all mammals. Their distinctive colors become brighter when they are excited. Cool!

Anglerfish [ang-gler-fish]

Anglerfish live in the deepest parts of the ocean where it is completely dark. Female Anglerfish generate their own light from the fleshy growth on their heads. They use this light to attract prey. Neat!

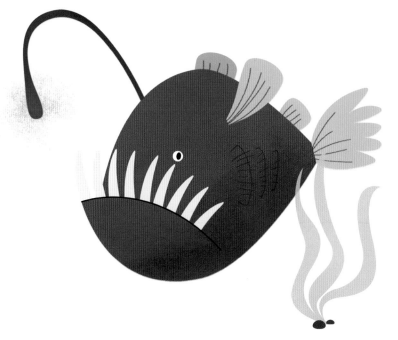